FORTUNE-TELLING
BOOK OF LOVE

This book belongs to

_____

The gift of

_____

K. C. Jones

Illustrations by Grady McFerrin

CHRONICLE BOOKS
SAN FRANCISCO

INTRO

What does your life hold for you when it comes to love? Many believe that love is preordained and that couples are destined to find one another. Others say that there is no such thing as one perfect match and love is simply a matter of timing. No matter which side you fall on, you should know that there are time-tested steps you can take to draw love in, determine if that love is true, and, once you have committed to love, keep the flames of connection and passion alight. Are you ready to begin? If so, read on . . .

CHAPTER 1:
LOOKING FOR LOVE

We all desire a deep, lasting, and true love. But wanting love is often far easier than finding it. Through the ages, men and women have used spells, potions, dreams, and omens to divine their love fortunes and create successful love matches for themselves and others. Let the wisdom of those who have gone before you serve as your guide when it comes to seeking—and finding—love.

SIGNS THAT LOVE IS ON ITS WAY

Stay alert! Signs of love are all around.

If any one of the following things happens, take it as a good love omen:

❖ If you stumble while ascending a flight of stairs, love will soon come to you.

❖ A man who wipes his hands on your apron while you are wearing it will fall irreversibly in love with you.

❖ Stockings that curl around each other while hanging on a clothesline are a sign that love is on its way into your life.

❖ If you hear a cricket chirp from the east, an old lover will soon return to you.

❖ If your nose itches, you have a secret admirer. You will need to use your powers of deduction to uncover his identity. If it is your right ear that is itching, your admirer is speaking well of you at that very moment.

❖ On New Year's Eve, throw your shoe into a willow tree. If it catches within the branches, you will be married within the year. (You may make nine attempts.)

❖ Finding bubbles floating in a noncarbonated drink spells forthcoming luck in love.

❖ If, while cooking or cleaning, you drop a pot or pan and it lands upside down on the floor, you will soon meet a new love.

❖ If a dog that does not belong to you follows you home, a new suitor will follow not long after.

❖ Finding a four-leaf clover augurs luck in life as well as in love: if you pluck one, expect love to follow. On the other hand, finding a one-leaf clover means you will soon receive a letter. Perhaps a love letter?

❖ Seeing a pair of birds next to each other on the same branch of a tree indicates that a new love will soon enter your life.

❖ Everyone knows that to have a black cat cross your path is a bad omen. However, if a tortoiseshell cat walks in front of you, rejoice, for love awaits!

❖ Seeing a new moon over your right shoulder on a Monday is a sure sign that love is on its way. However, if you go outside on the night of a new moon and deliberately look over your shoulder, it will jinx the luck; it must happen accidentally.

❖ Seeing a long-legged spider climb a wall in your bedroom may mean that love will soon be yours. However squeamish you may be, do not kill the spider, lest you destroy your luck!

RITUALS FOR A REQUITED LOVE

If you have your eye on a certain someone (or someones) and want to know if the love will be reciprocated, heed these signs:

❖ Before you go to bed at night, name the corners of your bedroom. The first corner you look upon when you wake the next morning indicates the person with whom you have the best chance of love.

❖ The next time you get the hiccups, think of the person you want to fall in love with you. If the hiccups stop within ten seconds, it augurs well for a relationship between the two of you. If they continue for longer, this person will never be your long-term mate.

❖ Take four onions, and on each one write the name of one person in whom you are interested. Put them under your bed and wait a full day. The onion that sprouts will be the person who will love you. If no onions sprout, you will have to look elsewhere for love.

❖ Write down the names of all your love interests, each on a separate piece of paper. Cut as many pieces of yarn as there are pieces of paper and tape or tie the pieces of paper to the strands of yarn. Place the pieces of paper in a bag, with the free ends of the yarn sticking out, and, closing your eyes, choose one piece of yarn. The name at the end of the yarn will be your future love.

LOVE OMENS IN NATURE

Harness the psychic qualities of the natural world to learn your love fortune. Keep your eyes open and pay close attention.

BUTTERFLIES

Butterflies are good omens for love; seeing a butterfly fluttering in the air or hovering over a plant or flower means a new love is about to come into your life. Though butterflies of all colors portend good luck, it is generally held that the brighter the butterfly, the better the love portent. No matter how captivating it may be, you should never try to chase or capture a butterfly. This will turn your luck from positive to negative.

FROGS

Frogs attract love and are said to carry the spirit of innocent love; seeing a frog in nature, especially by a body of water, bodes very well for your love life. Finding a frog in your house, though it may be startling, is also incredibly lucky for love. If you are not witnessing frogs in the natural world, you may be able to speed love's coming by placing frog figurines around your house or by wearing jewelry or clothing with frog motifs on them. Finding a dead frog means that somewhere nearby a love affair has ended.

GOOD LUCK SYMBOLS

Traditional symbols of good luck, such as four-leaf clovers, horseshoes, and lucky pennies may be directed to bring luck in love if treated properly. If you find one of these totems and wish to use its energy to bring love your way, bury it in a metal box in your garden. Each time you find a new good-luck symbol, add it to the box and watch your love grow.

KNOTS

Knots are symbols of love and connection. Thus, finding a knot occurring in the natural world or in your home, which you did not tie yourself, is a fortuitous omen. Finding knots in nature (for example, in the tendrils of a plant) holds the same portent. If you do find a knot, do not untie it, for this could reverse your luck. Instead, place the knot under the pillow of a person you wish to love you and do not be surprised if a romance blossoms.

LADYBUGS

Although ladybugs are best known for the luck they bring, they also are omens of love. If a ladybug lands on your hand, arm, or leg, do not brush it away but rather wait until it flies off on its own. If you are seeking love, the ladybug will fly away, go directly to the person who will be your next love, and whisper your name to him. The number of spots on the ladybug represents the number of weeks until you will meet your love.

BIRDS

Birds have the power to foretell the future. As they fly overhead, they can see everything. Watch their movements, and you may get a sense of what is coming in your love life. The flight pattern of the first bird you see when you go outside in the morning will give the most accurate results. Even if you do not like the answer you get, do not be tempted to seek a bird omen again until the following day.

❖ **If a bird flies right to left:** You will get what you want when it comes to love.

❖ **If a bird flies left to right:** Obstacles to love may be in the way. This does not mean you will not find love; it only means you must rethink your approach.

❖ **If you see a bird changing direction in mid-flight:** Be prepared to be flexible when it comes to love.

❖ **If you see a bird flying straight up:** This is a very good omen, as something momentous and unexpected is around the corner for you in love.

❖ **If you see a bird hovering in the air or fighting against the wind:** A suitor is not who he appears to be. Proceed with caution.

❖ **If you see a bird flying toward you:** Your love life will improve, and quickly.

❖ **If you see a bird flying directly away from you:** Delay any plans or trips for the next month and take some time to reevaluate what you want out of love. Sometimes being alone for a while is the best course of action.

The colors of birds also carry portents. Again, use only the first bird you see as an omen for your luck in love that day.

❖ **Red:** Good fortune is coming.

❖ **Orange:** Great happiness and exciting times await.

❖ **Yellow:** Be on guard for unexpected surprises in love.

❖ **Green:** There is an adventure ahead.

❖ **Blue:** You will have true love.

❖ **Gray:** Your next relationship will bring peace and contentment.

❖ **Brown:** An argument will be resolved without much difficulty.

❖ **Black:** Rocky times are ahead, but you will avoid lasting trouble.

❖ **White:** Happiness in love is on its way.

Specific bird species also carry omens.

❖ **Bluebird:** Your love will be a happy one.

❖ **Cardinal:** Life-changing events are on your love horizon.

❖ **Crane:** You will need to make a difficult relationship decision. Consult those whose wisdom you trust.

❖ **Crow:** Travel is in your future—perhaps a romantic getaway for two?

❖ **Dove:** The future looks bright.

❖ **Duck:** Your relationship will be a stable one. (If the duck is quacking, this is an even more positive omen.)

❖ **Eagle:** Your relationship will be marked by success in love as well as success in business affairs.

❖ **Hummingbird:** Your mate will be forever faithful.

❖ **Robin:** You will be lucky in love.

❖ **Sparrow:** You and your true love will always have a happy home.

❖ **Wren:** Though love matters may look bleak now, the situation will improve.

THE MEANING OF DREAMS

Dreams can be powerful predictors of love. Even though your conscious mind may not sense love in the air, your unconscious knows better. The presence of any of the following signs in your dreams speaks volumes about your love, be it past, current, or future. Heed them!

AMETHYST

If you have a dream in which you are holding or wearing an amethyst, you will be successful in love and will have a blissful and satisfying marriage.

ATTIC

If an attic appears in your dream, this augurs a successful marriage is in the future, although there may be a few obstacles to overcome to get there.

BABY

Seeing a baby or babies in your dream marks a new beginning is on the horizon—but not in the literal sense. More than likely, the new beginning means a new love affair.

BANJO

A banjo or guitar appearing in a dream signifies that you will enjoy the company of good friends. However, if the stringed instrument is being played, one of these good friends will become a love interest.

BATHTUB

If a bathtub makes an appearance in your dream, your subconscious is ready to receive love. Work to consciously exude this feeling, all the while keeping an eye out for potential suitors.

BED

If you dream you are making a bed, it is likely that a new love will soon be sharing your bed.

BIRD

Seeing a bird in your dream, especially if the bird is in flight, symbolizes a new love winging its way toward you, one that will be both balanced and harmonious. Seeing a bird's nest in your dream is also a positive sign, as it foretells new opportunities of all kinds, including in love.

BLANKET

Not surprisingly, a blanket appearing in a dream signifies
security, protection, warmth, and love. If you are wrapping
someone in a blanket in your dream, it means your heart is
open and you are ready to care deeply for another person.

BUCKET

A pail or bucket in a dream is an incredibly fortuitous sign.
At the very least, it signifies that there will be an improve-
ment in your love life. If the bucket is full, you will soon
find love as well as wealth. An empty bucket points to
overcoming a conflict in love and coming out stronger on
the other side.

CARDS

Seeing playing cards in your dream can signify that the
time is right to fall in love. If one of the cards is a heart,
happiness in love is in your future.

CHESS

If you are playing chess in your dream, or watching a
game of chess being played, this may mean that your current mate, or future mate, will be your true equal in life.

CLOVER

If you dream of clover, your marriage will be both happy and prosperous.

DANDELIONS

Dandelions in a dream augur happiness and comfort in love in the future.

DONKEY

If a donkey or mule shows up in your dream, and it is carrying a heavy load, this points to success in love for you.

ERRANDS

A dream in which you are running errands foretells a passionate love affair that is soon to come.

FAIR

Winning prizes at a state or county fair means that you will soon win the best prize of all: true love.

FAWN

A fawn in a dream augurs a coming love affair marked by fidelity on both sides.

FIRE

Dreaming of a fire in a fireplace means a passionate evening with a stranger will soon take place. However, do not look for this to turn into a lasting relationship.

FLOWERS

Dreaming that you are receiving flowers means that someone holds secret affection or admiration for you; keep your
eye out for a new suitor. A dream of flowers can also signify
that a rift in a current relationship will soon be healed.

FLUTE

If a flute appears in your dream, expect to be reunited with
an old flame soon.

GARDEN

A garden of beautiful flowers or well-tended vegetables
speaks of increased prosperity and true love in your future.

GIFT

If you dream that you are receiving a gift, this foretells an
upswing in your luck in love.

GLOVES

If you find or are given a pair of gloves in a dream, a new
love affair will soon be yours.

GONDOLA

If you dream you are riding in a gondola or other elevated vehicle, romance is on the horizon. Look for new love to appear soon, or for a resurgence of happy feelings in your current relationship.

ICE CREAM

Dreaming of ice cream points to happiness and success in love. If the ice cream is melting fast, it means that something momentous will happen soon in your love life.

LACE

If you are wearing lace in your dream, this means that what you desire in love will come to you. If someone else is wearing the lace, your next lover will always be faithful. If you or someone else is making lace, you will be married within the year.

LASSO

Swinging a lasso in a dream portends a love that is peaceful and content. If you are roping an animal with your lasso, you will meet your true love soon, and the love you feel will be returned in spades.

LEATHER

A dream in which you are wearing leather signifies luck in financial matters as well as good fortune in love.

MERRY-GO-ROUND

Dreaming that you are riding a merry-go-round or a carousel points to a new romantic love. Look around—your true love might be right in front of your eyes.

NECKLACE

A dream in which you are wearing a necklace, or in which someone puts a necklace on you, foretells a happy marriage full of unconditional love.

OTTER

Seeing an otter in your dream means you will always be happy in love and that your love will be marked by much laughter.

OX

If an ox appears in your dream, you are secretly admired by someone you know now only as a friend. If it is a pair of oxen you see, your marriage will be a strong and happy one.

PAN

A frying pan in a dream portends a complete and fulfilling love, either with your current partner or with a future mate.

POND

Dreaming of a clear pond means you will find love with someone who reciprocates your affection. If the pond has fish in it, chances are good that you and your love will also form a business relationship at some point in the future, and that the partnership will be a profitable one.

QUICKSAND

If you dream that you are rescued from quicksand, this means that a worthy lover will soon cross your path. Seize the moment!

RABBIT

A white rabbit in a dream stands for fidelity in love, while more than one rabbit could mean you will bear many children.

RAIN

Rain in a dream is a harbinger of forgiveness, renewal, and increased awareness in relationships. So if you are having love troubles and you dream of rain, those troubles may soon be resolved.

RAINBOW

Dreaming of a rainbow signifies happiness in love beyond all expectations.

RING

If you dream of wearing a ring, this is an indication of your commitment to a relationship, whether it be an existing one or a future one. If you are given a ring in your dream, your next lover will always be true.

ROSE

Dreaming of a blooming rose signifies the birth of a new love. It can also point to a marriage of true love. If you smell the rose in your dream, your new lover will always be faithful. A wild rosebush points to a family wedding occurring soon—perhaps it will be yours!

RUNNING

If, in your dream, you are running, you are likely on the brink of a big change in your life. A new love, perhaps? Keep your eyes peeled when you wake.

SEAL

Seals represent luck and security in love, as well as playfulness and spontaneity, so if one appears in your dream, prepare for some fun and adventure in your love life.

SPIDERS

Counterintuitively, spiders in a dream symbolize good luck. If the spider is spinning a web, look closely—if a letter appears in the web, it will be the first initial of your true love.

STARRY SKY

If you see a night sky filled with stars in your dream, this points to a long-lasting love and eventual happy marriage.

SWIMMING

A dream in which you are swimming is a good omen for love. If you are swimming in a pool, expect a welcome surprise in love in the next week. If you are swimming in open water, your love will thrive, and along with it will come increased wealth.

TORCH

If you are carrying a lit torch in your dream, you will find great love with a coworker or colleague.

VALENTINE

Seeing an old-fashioned valentine in a dream means that an old flame will reenter your life. Be prepared to make a choice.

VINEYARD

Dreaming of a vineyard symbolizes that you will have many prospects from which to choose when it comes to love.

WAND

If you are holding a wand in your dream, this signifies the power of your will when it comes to love. Never fear. You will get what you want.

YARN

A dream of yarn foretells that you will marry a very wealthy person.

YAWN

If in your dream you are yawning, this may mean that you have unrealistic expectations when it comes to love. True love is waiting for you, but first you must realize that nobody is perfect.

ZEBRA

A zebra in a dream means you will soon meet someone who is your opposite in almost every way. Despite your differences you will fall in love quickly, and fall hard.

SPELLS FOR LOVE

If you are not seeing signs of love occurring in the natural world or in your dreams, perhaps it is time to take matters into your own hands. Love spells have worked for centuries to attract love and ensure it is requited. For the best result, perform these spells when the moon is waxing (going from new to full), unless directed otherwise.

When casting spells for love, you must always believe that the spell will work. Doubting the power of magic will never make your wishes come true. Also, be aware that love spells cannot bewitch someone into falling in love with you—rather, a love spell performed correctly enhances your own magical energy so you attract the right person.

Certain days of the week are imbued with certain characteristics and are linked to ruling celestial bodies, which means there may be a day that is better than others for the type of spell you are trying to perform. Use the following chart as a guide.

DAY OF THE WEEK	RULING BODY	TYPE OF SPELL
Monday	The Moon	Spell for intuition in a relationship
Tuesday	Mars	Spell for increased passion
Wednesday	Mercury	Spell for better communication
Thursday	Jupiter	Spell for getting to the next step in a relationship
Friday	Venus	Spell for falling in love
Saturday	Saturn	Spell for more structure in a relationship
Sunday	The Sun	Spell for healing in a relationship

GODS AND GODDESSES OF LOVE

To amplify the power of love spells, invoke one or more of these deities while performing the spell.

- ❖ **Aizen-Myo-o:** Japanese (Buddhist) god of love

- ❖ **Ani-Ibo:** African goddess of happiness and love

- ❖ **Aphrodite:** Greek goddess of love

- ❖ **Branwyn:** Celtic goddess of love, sexuality, and the ocean

- ❖ **Cupid:** son of Venus; Roman god of love

- ❖ **Eros:** Greek god of love

- ❖ **Erzulie:** Voodoo goddess of love, passion, fertility, beauty, and sex

- ❖ **Freya:** Norse goddess of love, fertility, and beauty

- ❖ **Hathor:** Egyptian goddess of love, music, and joy

- ❖ **Inanna:** Sumerian goddess of love and war

- ❖ **Ishtar:** Babylonian goddess of love

- **Isis:** Egyptian goddess of fertility, motherhood, and magic

- **Juno:** Roman goddess of the moon; protector of women in labor

- **Kama:** Hindu god of love

- **Lakshmi:** Hindu goddess of beauty and fertility

- **Oshun:** Yoruban spirit-goddess of love, beauty, and intimacy

- **Radha:** Hindu goddess of love

- **Tlazolteotl:** Aztec goddess of love, fertility, sex, and childbirth

- **Venus:** Roman goddess of love and beauty

- **Xochipilli:** Aztec god of love

SPELLS TO ATTRACT LOVE

The following spells will bring new love into your life.

ROSE PETAL SPELL

You will need:

- ❖ A handful of rose petals procured from a friend or loved one

To perform the spell, hold the rose petals in your hand and walk one hundred steps from your front door. Turn around and walk back toward your front door, and, while you are walking, scatter the petals on the ground around you. As you do this, say out loud:

Love, find your way
Love, come to stay!

Repeat these words as you approach your door, until all the petals but one have been scattered. Hold the remaining petal and take it inside with you and put it by your bed. Be on the lookout as you return to your house over the week that follows. It is very possible that a new love will follow you home.

RED, RED HEART SPELL

You will need:

❖ Red paper

❖ Scissors

❖ Candle

❖ Matches

❖ An envelope

On the first day of the new moon, cut a heart shape from the paper. Light the candle, and, holding the heart shape and standing in front of the candle, repeat these words:

As this red heart glows by candlelight,
I draw love closer to me this night.

Place the heart in the envelope, and, using wax from the candle, seal it shut. Place the envelope in a safe place and do not look at it again until the next new moon, one month later. By this time, a love interest should have entered your life. If this has not occurred, repeat the ritual for one more month.

SALT AND PEPPER SHAKER SPELL

You will need:

❖ 16-in/40.5-cm length of red ribbon

❖ Salt shaker

❖ Pepper shaker

On a Friday morning, tie the ribbon to the salt and pepper shakers with loose knots, leaving about 12 in/30.5 cm of slack ribbon between them. The next morning, untie the knots, move the shakers 2 in/5 cm closer together, and retie the knots. Repeat this ritual until the shakers touch each other, and bind them by wrapping the ribbon around them twice and tying a knot. Leave the shakers tied together for one week. During this time, you should meet a new love.

DOUBLE TWIG SPELL

You will need:

❖ Two twigs, each about the same length and width

❖ Pencil or pen

❖ 8-in/20-cm length of twine

One twig represents you, and the other represents your next love. Write your name on one twig, and, on the other, write a few characteristics you are seeking in a mate.

Tie the twigs together with the twine so they are touching and see yourself in your mind's eye, standing next to a new love. Toss the twig bundle into a body of water and exclaim, "From now on, together!" Repeat the spell each week until a new love comes to you.

SPELLS FOR DREAMING OF LOVE

These spells will bring you images of your next lover while you sleep.

ROSEMARY AND THYME SHOE SPELL

This spell was traditionally performed on January 20, on the Eve of St. Agnes. But it will also work on the night a full moon appears.

You will need:

❖ One sprig rosemary

❖ One sprig thyme

❖ A pair of your shoes

❖ A small bowl of water

Before you go to sleep, put the sprig of rosemary in your left shoe and the sprig of thyme in your right shoe. Place the shoes where the light of the moon can fall upon them and sprinkle a few drops of water on the herbs in each shoe.

As you get in bed, chant this spell three times:

In the light of the moon, I work this old herbal spell.
By my will and desire, may it all turn out well.
A vision of my future love, reveal to me this night;
A dream conjured from rosemary, thyme, and moonlight.

When you wake the next day, write down any dreams that you had. Dispose of the rosemary and thyme outdoors, and pay attention to any new love interests who enter your life from now until the next full moon comes around.

MARJORAM, VIOLET, AND ROSE SPELL

For the best results, perform this spell on a Friday under a full moon.

You will need:

❖ Marjoram

❖ Violet petals (fresh or dried)

❖ Rose petals (fresh or dried)

❖ A small sachet

Combine a small amount of marjoram, violet petals, and rose petals in the sachet. Go outside and hold out the bag up into the moonlight, saying:

Marjoram, tucked in a sweet-smelling sachet,
Chase away the blues and keep bad dreams away.
Add violets for the lady, and the rose for love.
Hear me, Aphrodite, and answer from above.

Go inside and place the sachet under your pillow. Just before you retire for the night, say the following words:

Oh, enchanted herbs so sweet,
Bring to me dreams of the man I am to meet.

SPELLS TO WIN THE LOVE OF SOMEONE YOU DESIRE

If you have met someone you want to be your love, or if you have your eye on a certain someone but are not sure the feeling is requited, use these spells to hasten your prospect's affections.

ROSE AND CANDLE SPELL

Perform this spell in the evening before bedtime.

You will need:

❖ A red rose

❖ Two large red candles

❖ Matches

Arrange the rose and candles on a table by your bedside, putting the rose between the candles. Do not light the candles yet. Go to sleep. At sunrise the next morning, sit by an open window that faces east. Hold the rose and recite these words:

This red rose is for true love.
True love, come, come to me.

Return the rose to its place on the table. Light both candles, and, as you look into their flames, visualize love growing in the heart of your intended. Keep the candles lit for a full day and night or until the rose begins to wilt. Bury the rose in a sunny spot.

BLOOMING BULB SPELL

You will need:

- A flower bulb or plant bulb

- A pencil or pen

- An earthen pot

- Potting soil

Write the name of your desired on the bulb you have chosen, be it a flower bulb like tulip, daffodil, or hyacinth, or an edible bulb like onion, shallot, or garlic. Plant the bulb in a new pot and place it so it faces the dwelling of the one you want to love you. Care for the bulb as directed. Each day, until the bulb first sends up green shoots, repeat this spell:

May its roots grow,
May its leaves grow,
May its flowers grow,
And as it does, so may
[the name of your desired]'s love for me grow.

SEED AND PENNY SPELL

You will need:

❖ Potting soil

❖ An earthen pot

❖ A new penny

❖ A packet of seeds (herbs work well)

Place soil in the pot until it is two-thirds full. Go outside one clear night when the moon is out and hold a shiny new penny up, facing the moonlight. Then, bury the penny in the soil. Next, arrange the seeds atop the soil so they form the initial of your desired's first name. Cover the seeds with a half-inch of soil and sprinkle with water.

As the seeds sprout and grow, so will love. Keep the pot in sunlight during the day and in moonlight during the night. The copper in the penny and the forces of the sun and moon will work together to draw love to you.

LOVE POTIONS

Potions are powerful tools that can enhance spells or be used on their own to create love where none existed before. They can be essential oil mixtures, used in conjunction with candles for maximum effect, or decoctions or other edibles taken by mouth.

CLARY SAGE POTION

This essential oil combination can be used to draw a new lover to you, or it can enhance harmony in an existing relationship.

You will need:

❖ 3 drops clary sage oil

❖ 1 drop sandalwood oil

❖ 1 drop ylang-ylang oil

❖ A small bowl

❖ A pink or red candle

❖ Matches

Stir the oils together in the bowl and then rub the mixture all over the candle. Light the candle and burn for three hours. Be careful to gently snuff out the flame, as blowing out the candle will blow your wishes away. Repeat each day as necessary until the desired result is achieved.

CITRUS POTION

This essential-oil recipe is best used when you have a lover in mind but that person thinks of you only as a friend.

You will need:

❖ 3 drops lavender oil

❖ 1 drop lemon oil

❖ 3 drops orange or tangerine oil

❖ A small bowl

❖ A candle of any color

❖ Matches

Stir the oils together in the bowl and then rub the mixture over the candle. Light the candle and say the name of your love interest three times out loud. Let the candle burn for three hours before you snuff it out. To heighten the effect of this potion, you may also light the candle when you and your love interest are together (but you must not say why you are performing the ritual!).

FLOWER HERB POTION

Mix up this potion before you pay a visit to the person you wish to be your lover.

You will need:

❖ Small bunch marigold

❖ Small bunch lavender

❖ Small bunch rosemary

❖ Mortar and pestle

❖ A shallow dish

Place the herbs in the light of a full moon for three hours. Next (and this can be done the following day), strip or pluck the soft leaves and petals from the stems of the herbs and flowers. Using the mortar and pestle, muddle the leaves together until their fragrance is released. Transfer the concoction to the shallow dish and place in a room where you know your love interest will be spending time.

GEMSTONES FOR LOVE

Gems and semiprecious stones may also be used in spells and rituals to attract and foretell love.

ROSE QUARTZ SPELL

You will need:

❖ Four candles

❖ A table and chair

❖ Matches

❖ A piece of rose quartz

Place the candles on the table at due north, due south, due east, and due west. Light them. Hold the rose quartz in your hands and sit in a chair, facing the table. Close your eyes and repeat the following:

As the room fills with the energy of this stone,
May love fill my life so I may not be alone.

Then place the rose quartz on the table in the middle of the candles and say:

New love, enter into my world and into my heart.
New love, let us never be apart.

Gently snuff out the candles and let the candles and quartz sit on the table overnight.

Gemstones also have divinatory meaning. For a quick answer about your love fortune, place a selection of different gems in a bag. Concentrate on your question and then shake out a stone at random from the bag. If two fall out, look at both meanings.

- **Agate:** A pleasant surprise awaits you.

- **Amethyst:** Your love will be faithful and free from jealousy.

- **Clear quartz:** Your love will have staying power.

- **Emerald:** A secret admirer desires you.

- **Garnet:** A love letter is on its way!

- **Hematite:** New opportunities in love beckon. Do not let them pass you by.

- **Jade:** Your need for perfection will hinder you when it comes to love.

- **Opal:** A love affair will end.

- **Rose quartz:** Love will arrive in an unexpected form.

- ❖ **Ruby:** Power and passion will be intertwined in your next relationship.

- ❖ **Sapphire:** Your past will catch up with you.

- ❖ **Sardonyx:** A wedding is coming.

- ❖ **Snowflake obsidian:** You are nearing the end of a challenging time in love.

- ❖ **Snow quartz:** A profound change in love will soon happen.

- ❖ **Tigereye:** All is not as it appears to be; proceed with caution.

- ❖ **Turquoise:** You will soon embark on a journey of love.

TAROT FOR LOVE

Tarot cards may be used on their own or in conjunction with spells to draw love to you.

While tarot cups cards are most commonly used in spells for general love, you can intensify the power of spells (including the one on the facing page) by choosing a suit that corresponds directly with the astrological sign of the person you wish to love you.

IF THE OBJECT OF YOUR AFFECTION IS:	CHOOSE:
Aries, Leo, Sagittarius	Wands
Pisces, Cancer, Scorpio	Cups
Taurus, Virgo, Capricorn	Pentacles
Gemini, Libra, Aquarius	Swords

TAROT CUPS SPELL

In the tarot, the suit of cups represents matters of love and the heart, hence the use of this suit in the spell. The king of any suit represents the male, while the queen represents the female. And the nine is the card for wishes. This spell will help attract the object of your affection to you. Perform it on a Friday evening during a waxing moon.

You will need:

❖ A deck of tarot cards

❖ A red, orange, or pink candle (red represents passion, pink love, and orange balance, so choose whichever one best suits your desired outcome)

❖ Orange oil

❖ Matches

Take the king, queen, and nine of cups from your deck of tarot cards. Place them in front of you. Next, anoint the candle with the orange oil. Light the candle, and while you gaze into its flame, imagine you and your potential love drawing close together. (If you can perform this ritual while your intended love is in the house, all the better.) Snuff out the candle when you are finished.

Perform this exact ritual again on the night of the next full moon. Repeat as necessary during the next moon cycle.

PLAYING CARDS FOR LOVE PORTENTS

Cartomancy is the art of using playing cards for divination, and can be used to read love fortunes. The easiest way to use cartomancy for love is to pull one card per day from a full deck and then heed its portent.

Each suit in a deck of cards is associated with a particular element:

❖ **Clubs:** Fire

❖ **Spades:** Air

❖ **Hearts:** Water

❖ **Diamonds:** Earth

Clubs signify business, ambition, creativity, and personal initiative.

Spades signify gossip, challenges, wisdom, and warning.

Hearts signify love, friendship, femininity, happiness, and domestic concerns.

Diamonds signify career, money, materialism, and clarity.

Another way to use playing cards to divine your love fortune is to shuffle the cards, draw three cards out of the deck
at random, and lay them facedown in front of you in a line.
Then turn them over, one by one. The first card you turn
over represents your past in love, the second your present,
and the third your future. Use the same portents as listed
on the following pages.

CLUBS

❖ **2**: Hurtful gossip about your relationship is swirling around you; do not fall prey to it.

❖ **3**: A proposal or proposition of some sort is augured. If you are hoping to get engaged, take special note. And if you are married, it is also a fortuitous omen.

❖ **4**: Beware of people who may be deceitful. If something seems too good to be true, it probably is.

❖ **5**: A new relationship will begin, but most likely it will be a friendship rather than a love affair.

❖ **6**: Success in money will be followed by success in love.

❖ **7**: Success will come, but it will more likely be in business than in love.

❖ **8**: Troubled times at work lie ahead, but it will be smooth sailing for you in love.

❖ **9**: You will meet a wealthy person; or the one you are involved with will come into money unexpectedly.

❖ **10**: Someone you met on a vacation in your past will resurface and may turn into a new love for you.

❖ **Jack**: A dark-haired man will come into your life.

❖ **Queen**: A dark-haired woman will give you good advice on love.

❖ **King**: You will encounter a generous man with a lively spirit.

❖ **Ace**: You will gain sudden happiness in love, but do not become too attached, for it may be fleeting.

SPADES

❖ **2**: Someone you are interested in has problems with fidelity.

❖ **3**: A third person will enter your relationship.

❖ **4**: You will be confronted with small obstacles in love but do not take them too seriously. You will overcome them.

❖ **5**: Something will happen in love that will seem negative but turn out to be a blessing in disguise.

❖ **6**: Small changes are coming that will lead to big improvements.

❖ **7**: You will receive love advice, but you should disregard it, no matter how forcefully it is pressed upon you.

❖ **8**: You will be tempted when it comes to love. Do not fall prey to it if you are in a relationship.

❖ **9**: A run of bad luck in love is coming. If you are single, stay that way.

❖ **10**: You need not worry so much when it comes to love.

❖ **Jack**: A young man will be jealous of attention you are receiving from others. Consider him as a prospect as well.

❖ **Queen**: A widowed woman will come into your life.

❖ **King**: You will meet an ambitious man, but he will not put you first.

❖ **Ace**: The end of a relationship is on the horizon; the relationship may be yours or that of someone very close to you.

HEARTS

❖ **2**: This card portends a great deal of strength and support, either from a current partner or from a new love interest.

❖ **3**: You may feel indecisive about your love life.

❖ **4**: Travel is in your future; do not let it disrupt a budding relationship.

❖ **5**: An old flame is jealous of your current situation.

❖ **6**: You will find love when you least expect to. Do not let it slip through your fingers.

❖ **7**: Someone you are interested in will prove unreliable.

❖ **8**: You will receive an invitation to a party; take it.

❖ **9**: A wish for love will come true!

❖ **10**: Good fortune in love awaits you after difficulty.

- ❖ **Jack**: You have a secret admirer who is younger than you.

- ❖ **Queen**: An older woman will help you or give you love advice.

- ❖ **King**: A kind man will enter your life.

- ❖ **Ace**: A love letter will arrive, and your worries will subside.

DIAMONDS

❖ **2**: A change in your relationship status is on the horizon.

❖ **3**: You will need to take the high road and use tact to avoid a lover's quarrel.

❖ **4**: You will receive love advice from a relative or colleague; do not disregard it.

❖ **5**: It is a good time to start new projects of any kind—even in love!

❖ **6**: This card portends dissent and arguments. Tread lightly in love.

❖ **7**: An argument will be resolved to your satisfaction.

❖ **8**: Something new is on the horizon—either a new job or a new love. You cannot have both.

❖ **9**: You will feel restless in love. Be patient, and the feeling will pass.

❖ **10**: A change for the better, whether in money or love.

❖ **Jack**: A jealous person is in your midst; he or she wants what you have in love.

❖ **Queen**: A female acquaintance will spread gossip about your love life.

❖ **King**: A blond or gray-haired man will come into your life.

❖ **Ace**: Good news will arrive in the form of change. Use it to your advantage.

ASTROLOGY FOR LOVE

When looking for love, astrology can give you answers about courting your perfect zodiac match.

IF YOUR DESIRED MATE'S BIRTH-DAY FALLS ON OR BETWEEN THESE DATES . . .*	HIS OR HER ASTROLOGICAL SIGN IS . . .
March 22–April 21	Aries
April 22–May 21	Taurus
May 22–June 21	Gemini
June 22–July 21	Cancer
July 22–August 21	Leo
August 22–September 21	Virgo
September 22–October 21	Libra
October 22–November 21	Scorpio
November 22–December 21	Sagittarius
December 22–January 21	Capricorn
January 22–February 21	Aquarius
February 22–March 21	Pisces

*If the birthday is two to three days from the beginning or end of a date range, that person is "on the cusp," meaning that he or she may also display characteristics of the sign that precedes or follows the corresponding sign.

ARIES

An Aries person is independent, optimistic, courageous, and generous but can be impatient and short-tempered.

Aries enjoys the chase and sometimes can see love as a conquest to be won. When wooing an Aries, keep this in mind and let Aries make the first move. Seeing yourself as a prize to be attained can do wonders for your ego. If you play this right, once Aries has committed, the relationship will be forever interesting, fresh, and passionate.

This pairing works well if you are a:

Leo or Sagittarius

Avoid this pairing if you are a:

Cancer, Libra, or Capricorn

TAURUS

✧ Birthday: April 22–May 21 ✧

A Taurus person is loyal, dependable, patient, and generous but can also be stubborn and possessive.

Taurus is easygoing, straightforward, stable, and reliable, so if you wish to court a Taurus, know that you do not need to put on a big show. The simple pleasures of life and love—quiet nights at home, long talks, quality time spent together—suit Taurus just fine, even at the very beginning of a relationship. Taurus also expects loyalty in love and can sniff out insincerity, so if you really want your Taurus, do not date around.

This pairing works well if you are a:

Virgo or Capricorn

Avoid this pairing if you are a:

Leo, Scorpio, or Aquarius

GEMINI

❖ Birthday: May 22–June 21 ❖

Gemini is witty, imaginative, energetic, and adaptable but can also be fickle, restless, and indecisive.

To woo a Gemini, you must never be boring. Embrace spontaneity and get ready to try new things. Gemini wears his heart on his sleeve and will expect the same from you—be prepared to share what is on your mind. However, if you are looking for stability and deep emotional support in the early stages of a relationship, you had best look elsewhere.

This pairing works well if you are a:

Libra or Aquarius

Avoid this pairing if you are a:

Virgo, Sagittarius, or Pisces

CANCER

❖ Birthday: June 22–July 21 ❖

A Cancer individual is perceptive, caring, loyal, and dependable but can be moody, oversensitive, and clingy.

Cancer is empathetic, patient, nurturing, and kind when it comes to love. To woo a Cancer, you must submit to his need to protect and care for a mate to a degree that some may find stifling. If you pride yourself on your independent nature, you and Cancer may not be a match.

This pairing works well if you are a:

Scorpio or Pisces

Avoid this pairing if you are an:

Aries, Libra, or Capricorn

LEO

Leo is ambitious, generous, and confident but can also be vain, dramatic, and domineering.

Leo craves attention, so if you are trying to win her heart, grand gestures of love and affection are the best way to go. You must also be prepared to relinquish the spotlight and let her dominant personality shine through. But once won over, Leo will be romantic, idealistic, and loyal.

This pairing works well if you are an:

Aries or Sagittarius

Avoid this pairing if you are a:

Taurus, Scorpio, or Aquarius

VIRGO

❖ Birthday: August 22–September 21 ❖

Virgos are organized, reliable, and analytical, though they can also be particular to a fault, rigid, and skeptical.

Virgo is selective and slow to trust, so if you wish to woo her, be patient and steadfast. Once she finds her match, however, her affections are always genuine, and she will nurture and support you through good times and bad.

This pairing works well if you are a:

Taurus or Capricorn

Avoid this pairing if you are a:

Gemini, Sagittarius, or Pisces

LIBRA

A Libra is idealistic, diplomatic, and a seeker of peace. On the other hand, he can be indecisive, superficial, and vain.

Libra is on a lifelong quest for the perfect person who can complete him. To win his heart, you must prove yourself in the face of his innate idealism and indecision. Be confident in your feelings, and you will win him over. And once in love, your relationship will be harmonious.

This pairing works well if you are a:

Gemini or Aquarius

Avoid this pairing if you are an:

Aries, Cancer, or Capricorn

SCORPIO

❖ Birthday: October 22–November 21 ❖

Scorpios are passionate, curious, loyal, and resourceful. However, they can also be jealous, prone to obsession, and inflexible.

Scorpio's passion burns bright, so to woo him, you must try to match that passion. Scorpio is also a natural skeptic, so you will need to work hard to earn his trust. Once you do so, Scorpio will be unendingly faithful and committed but also prone to jealousy. And if you try to control Scorpio, you will be stung.

This pairing works well if you are a:

Cancer or Pisces

Avoid this pairing if you are a:

Taurus, Leo, or Aquarius

SAGITTARIUS

❖ **Birthday: November 22–December 21** ❖

The Sagittarius person is fun-loving and caring and an independent spirit who also has a strong intellectual streak. However, she can also be gullible and is prone to mood swings.

Sagittarius is honest and forthright at all costs, so from the beginning it is imperative that you not sugarcoat things. Also be careful not to be at all possessive, lest your Sagittarius slip through your fingers. If you play your cards right, you will reap the benefits of Sagittarius's humor and fun, and you will never be bored.

This pairing works well if you are an:

Aries or Leo

Avoid this pairing if you are a:

Gemini, Virgo, or Pisces

CAPRICORN

❖ Birthday: December 22–January 21 ❖

Capricorn is ambitious, responsible, loyal, and patient. She can also be self-absorbed and distrusting.

Capricorn fears rejection, so to win her heart, tell her how you feel on a regular basis. She thrives on committed relationships and will take her responsibility as one half of a couple very seriously, so to be her mate, you must be as practical, reliable, and stable as she is.

This pairing works well if you are a:

Taurus or Virgo

Avoid this pairing if you are a:

Aries, Cancer, or Libra

AQUARIUS

❖ **Birthday: January 22–February 21** ❖

Aquarius is a true original, with a forward-thinking nature that is often misunderstood by those around him. He is witty and humanitarian but can also be aloof, stubborn, and rebellious.

A mate's intelligence, not her physical appearance, is the most important criterion for an Aquarius. So you need not spend extra time on your looks to gain the love of an Aquarius; rather, be prepared for intellectual discussion and debate. If you thrive on this kind of academic exchange, you and Aquarius may be a good match.

This pairing works well if you are a:

Gemini or Libra

Avoid this pairing if you are a:

Taurus, Leo, or Scorpio

PISCES

❖ Birthday: February 22–March 21 ❖

A Pisces person is imaginative, compassionate, and tolerant but can also be oversensitive and lazy.

Pisces is devoted when it comes to love, so if you want a Pisces to be your mate, make sure he knows you are playing for keeps. Once he sees you are committed, he is more inclined to commit to you. If you sense hesitation from your Pisces, be gentle yet persistent with your affections, and more than likely he will come around.

This pairing works well if you are a:

Cancer or Scorpio

Avoid this pairing if you are a:

Gemini, Virgo, or Sagittarius

COMPATIBILITY CHART

Use this chart for an at-a-glance understanding of which signs make the best love matches and which do not. Check marks denote recommended pairings while Xs mark signs that are considered incompatible in love.

	Aries	Taurus	Gemini	Cancer	Leo	Virgo	Libra	Scorpio	Sagittarius	Capricorn	Aquarius	Pisces
Aries				✗	✓		✗		✓	✗		
Taurus				✗	✓		✗		✓	✗		
Gemini					✗	✓		✗			✓	✗
Cancer	✗						✗	✓		✗		✓
Leo	✓	✗						✗	✓		✗	
Virgo		✓	✗						✗	✓		✗
Libra	✗		✓	✗						✗	✓	
Scorpio		✗		✓	✗						✗	✓
Sagittarius	✓		✗		✓	✗						✗
Capricorn	✗	✓		✗		✓	✗					
Aquarius		✗	✓		✗		✓	✗				
Pisces			✗	✓		✗		✓	✗			

THE CHINESE ZODIAC FOR LOVE

Using the Chinese zodiac (an astrological system based on birth year) is another way to divine who your best love matches will be—and which signs are not a good fit.

IF YOUR DESIRED MATE WAS BORN IN …	HIS OR HER CHINESE ZODIAC ANIMAL IS …
1912, 1924, 1936, 1948, 1960, 1972, 1984, 1996, 2008, 2020	Rat
1913, 1925, 1937, 1949, 1961, 1973, 1985, 1997, 2009	Ox
1914, 1926, 1938, 1950, 1962, 1974, 1986, 1998, 2010	Tiger
1915, 1927, 1939, 1951, 1963, 1975, 1987, 1999, 2011	Rabbit
1916, 1928, 1940, 1952, 1964, 1976, 1988, 2000, 2012	Dragon
1917, 1929, 1941, 1953, 1965, 1977, 1989, 2001, 2013	Snake
1918, 1930, 1942, 1954, 1966, 1978, 1990, 2002, 2014	Horse
1919, 1931, 1943, 1955, 1967, 1979, 1991, 2003, 2015	Ram (Sheep or Goat)
1920, 1932, 1944, 1956, 1968, 1980, 1992, 2004, 2016	Monkey
1921, 1933, 1945, 1957, 1969, 1981, 1993, 2005, 2017	Rooster
1922, 1934, 1946, 1958, 1970, 1982, 1994, 2006, 2018	Dog
1923, 1935, 1947, 1959, 1971, 1983, 1995, 2007, 2019	Pig

RAT

Rat is charming and funny but can also be selfish, and can have a short fuse when provoked.

Rats enjoy social activities and being surrounded by a large circle of people. To win a Rat's heart, you will need to stand out from the crowd. Put your natural charm on display and let your true personality shine through, and your Rat will be sure to notice you.

This pairing works well if you are a:

Dragon or Monkey

Avoid this pairing if you are a:

Horse

OX

The Ox is patient and kind. He is very methodical in everything he does but can take this to the extreme and become self-absorbed, blocking out the world around him.

If you wish to woo an Ox, you need to understand that small talk and flirting may only make him uncomfortable. Get him alone and get right to the point. Tell him you have feelings for him and see how he responds.

This pairing works well if you are a:

Snake or Rooster

Avoid this pairing if you are a:

Ram

TIGER

Tiger is fearless, passionate, and intense. This intensity can translate into moodiness at times, however.

If the object of your affection is a Tiger, you will need to employ your best powers of seduction. Set the scene for romance and show Tiger that you can match her passion with your own.

This pairing works well if you are a:

Horse or Dog

Avoid this pairing if you are a:

Monkey

RABBIT

Rabbit is gentle, kind, soft-spoken, and nurturing. However, she avoids conflict at all costs and does not get along well with volatile personalities.

It may seem counterintuitive, but to make a Rabbit your mate, tap into her compassionate side and let her help you or take care of you. You will quickly discover if you are a good match.

This pairing works well if you are a:

Ram or Pig

Avoid this pairing if you are a:

Rooster

DRAGON

Dragons are independent personalities who like to do things their own way. They are quick to anger and can exact swift revenge when they or their loved ones are wronged.

Dragons have no problem producing fireworks in the early stages of a relationship but have more trouble with staying power when the embers of early love die down. To woo a Dragon, you must match his ardor but also prove to him that you can provide the affection and companionship that come with lasting true love.

This pairing works well if you are a:

Monkey or Rat

Avoid this pairing if you are a:

Dog

SNAKE

Snakes are intelligent and dedicated to their work. They tend to keep most of their feelings to themselves, but, when betrayed, they make fearsome enemies.

Snakes are the best-looking of all the signs and so attract love interests easily. However, under the surface they are quite insecure. To stand out from the crowd, you will need to appeal to a Snake's vanity and reassure him of his charms.

This pairing works well if you are a:

Rooster or Ox

Avoid this pairing if you are a:

Pig

HORSE

The Horse is magnetic, caring, and adventurous. However, she can be self-reliant to a fault and impatient with others.

To win the love of a Horse, you must show her that you can keep up with her physically and intellectually. A horse thrives on excitement and adventure in a relationship, so embrace spontaneity, even if you are more of a planner by nature.

This pairing works well if you are a:

Tiger or Dog

Avoid this pairing if you are a:

Rat

RAM

Ram is an extremely creative thinker, but along with these creative energies he sometimes possesses an insecurity that needs to be soothed.

Ram is a more private personality, so if you want to make him your mate, you must make a concerted effort to get to know him. Once he feels that you truly care for him, he will open up.

This pairing works well if you are a:

Rabbit or Pig

Avoid this pairing if you are an:

Ox

MONKEY

Monkey is a good listener with an empathetic personality but can be a bit fickle.

To woo a Monkey will take some energy. She is easily bored, so you must be constantly willing to try new things to keep her interested. Long-term relationships are not a Monkey's forte. If you want a mate for life, you will need to work on Monkey's staying power.

This pairing works well if you are a:

Dragon or Rat

Avoid this pairing if you are a:

Tiger

ROOSTER

Rooster is straightforward, direct, and honest. She is also analytical and shrewd in business matters but cannot resist a bit of boasting now and again about her talents.

To make a Rooster your mate, you must be thick-skinned. If you can handle her directness, you will realize that under Rooster's gruff exterior lies a heart full of love.

This pairing works well if you are a:

Snake or Ox

Avoid this pairing if you are a:

Rabbit

DOG

The Dog is slow to trust, though when he does feel comfortable with others, he will be loyal until the end. What may come across as a judgmental or critical nature is merely Dog's defense mechanism.

To win the heart of a Dog, move slowly and carefully and make it clear that you want to commit to him. Building his trust should be your goal.

This pairing works well if you are a:

Tiger or Horse

Avoid this pairing if you are a:

Dragon

PIG

A Pig has nothing to hide—what you see is what you get. Though Pig is a perfectionist, she is also very tolerant of others' foibles and differences.

Wooing a Pig should not be difficult, as she is one of the most open, affectionate, and understanding signs in the zodiac. But since Pig is amiable with almost everyone, it cannot hurt to make it clear to her that you want to be more than friends.

This pairing works well if you are a:

Ram or Rabbit

Avoid this pairing if you are a:

Snake

COMPATIBILITY CHART

Use this chart for an at-a-glance understanding of which signs make the best love matches and which do not. Check marks denote recommended pairings while Xs mark signs that are considered incompatible in love.

	Rat	Ox	Tiger	Rabbit	Dragon	Snake	Horse	Ram	Monkey	Rooster	Dog	Pig
Rat					✓		✗		✓			
Ox						✓		✗		✓		
Tiger							✓		✗		✓	
Rabbit								✓		✗		✓
Dragon	✓								✓		✗	
Snake		✓								✓		✗
Horse	✗		✓								✓	
Ram		✗		✓								✓
Monkey	✓		✗		✓							
Rooster		✓		✗		✓						
Dog			✓		✗		✓					
Pig				✓		✗		✓				

NATIVE AMERICAN ASTROLOGY
FOR LOVE

Native American tribes have their own astrological system, and its teachings offer wisdom on how each animal sign behaves in love.

IF YOUR DESIRED MATE'S BIRTHDAY FALLS ON OR BETWEEN THESE DATES . . .	HIS OR HER ASTROLOGICAL SIGN IS . . .
January 20–February 18	Otter
February 19–March 20	Wolf
March 21–April 19	Falcon
April 20–May 20	Beaver
May 21–June 20	Deer
June 21–July 21	Woodpecker
July 22–August 21	Salmon
August 22–September 21	Bear
September 22–October 22	Raven
October 23–November 22	Snake
November 23–December 21	Owl
December 22–January 19	Goose

* If a birthday is two to three days from the beginning or end of a date range, that person is "on the cusp," meaning that he or she may also display characteristics of the sign that precedes or follows the corresponding sign.

OTTER

Otter is perceptive and intuitive, with a great intelligence that she keeps hidden. If she is maligned or feels threatened, she will likely rebel and isolate herself from others.

To win the love of an Otter, you will need to dig below the surface—she does not open up easily. Be patient, and, if you can prove to her that you are around to stay, she will accept you.

This pairing works well if you are a:

Falcon, Deer, or Raven

Avoid this pairing if you are a:

Beaver, Salmon, or Snake

WOLF

The Wolf has a gentle and generous spirit, though he can become restless if not allowed to express his innate independence.

If you are trying to woo a Wolf, you must also allow him space to breathe. Let him take the lead in planning dates, and you will find him affectionate and compassionate—a near-perfect mate.

This pairing works well if you are a:

Woodpecker, Bear, or Snake

Avoid this pairing if you are a:

Deer or Owl

FALCON

❖ Birthday: March 21–April 19 ❖

Falcon is quick to action—when she sees something (or someone) she wants, she goes after it and usually gets it. She prefers partners and friends who will let her light shine a bit brighter than theirs, however, and can tend toward arrogance.

To win the heart of a Falcon, keep in mind that she prefers to take the initiative. Express your interest but then sit back and let her take control. If you do this, Falcon will surprise you with her passion and ardor.

This pairing works well if you are an:

Otter, Salmon, or Owl

Avoid this pairing if you are a:

Woodpecker, Raven, or Goose

BEAVER

The Beaver has a great ability to adapt to any situation, and possesses an unparalleled mental acuity. However, he can be somewhat less than tactful at times.

You will need a thick skin if you hope to make a mate of a Beaver; though he means well, he often speaks without thinking. If you can put up with this, you will find Beaver a loyal partner.

This pairing works well if you are a:

Woodpecker, Bear, or Goose

Avoid this pairing if you are an:

Otter, Salmon, or Snake

DEER

❖ Birthday: May 21–June 20 ❖

The Deer is the wittiest sign of the zodiac and a lively conversationalist. She may also be selfish and prone to narcissism and vanity, however.

To woo a Deer, you must be prepared to stroke her ego a bit. In return, she will keep you laughing and will inspire you to achieve great things.

This pairing works well if you are an:

Otter or Raven

Avoid this pairing if you are a:

Wolf, Bear, or Owl

WOODPECKER

Woodpecker is a caring sign, liking nothing more than to provide for her friends and loved ones. With no one to care for, she can find herself somewhat lost and aimless.

To win the heart of a Woodpecker, be prepared to dote on her and cater to her every whim until she finds her footing in the relationship. You will reap the benefits: later, she will return the nurturing in spades.

This pairing works well if you are a:

Wolf, Beaver, or Snake

Avoid this pairing if you are a:

Falcon, Raven, or Goose

SALMON

✤ Birthday: July 22–August 21 ✤

The Salmon is full of energy and a born motivator, though some may find him overly intense.

To win a Salmon's heart, make it a point to get one-on-one time with him. In a group situation, he will not single out any one person, and you will be overlooked.

This pairing works well if you are a:

Falcon or Owl

Avoid this pairing if you are an:

Otter, Beaver, or Snake

BEAR

The Bear is the most stable of all the zodiac signs. He is level-headed and reasonable, and generous, patient, and full of heart. However, he can be reclusive and withdrawn if things are not going well for him.

To woo a Bear, you will have to make the first move. Do not take his natural shyness as a sign that he is not interested.

This pairing works well if you are a:

Wolf, Beaver, or Goose

Avoid this pairing if you are a:

Deer or Owl

RAVEN

❖ Birthday: September 22–October 22 ❖

The Raven is charming, a true romantic, and attracts love easily, but can be hot-tempered.

Ravens prefer to do their own wooing rather than be wooed. With her strong intuition, Raven will know instinctively if a potential partner is not right for her. If she feels the two of you are not a good match, she will let you know.

This pairing works well if you are an:

Otter or Deer

Avoid this pairing if you are a:

Falcon, Woodpecker, or Goose

SNAKE

The Snake is the most mysterious of all the zodiac signs, with a dark energy and an intensity that scares many people away.

Winning a Snake's heart can be a difficult endeavor. He is slow to open up, and it takes him time to trust a partner. Tread lightly and do not come on too strong, lest Snake slip away.

This pairing works well if you are a:

Wolf or Woodpecker

Avoid this pairing if you are an:

Otter, Beaver, or Salmon

OWL

Owl is easygoing and adventurous, though some calmer spirits may find her reckless and excessive.

To woo an Owl, suggest active dates that may feel a bit risky; skydiving, race-car driving, and other similar pursuits will appeal to an Owl's sense of adventure.

This pairing works well if you are a:

Falcon or Salmon

Avoid this pairing if you are a:

Wolf, Deer, or Bear

GOOSE

Goose is a career-oriented sign, destined to succeed in business at all costs. Some may find him ruthless.

To win over a Goose, you must allow him space to concentrate on work matters. Even when he is smitten, he finds it impossible to lose himself completely in love. If you can support his business aims, he will shine and excel beyond even his own expectations and in turn can be a passionate and devoted partner.

This pairing works well if you are a:

Beaver or Bear

Avoid this pairing if you are a:

Falcon, Woodpecker, or Raven

COMPATIBILITY CHART

Use this chart for an at-a-glance understanding of which signs make the best love matches and which do not. Check marks denote recommended pairings while Xs mark signs that are considered incompatible in love.

	Otter	Wolf	Falcon	Beaver	Deer	Woodpecker	Salmon	Bear	Raven	Snake	Owl	Goose
Otter			✓	✗	✓		✗		✓	✗		
Wolf					✗	✓		✓		✓	✗	
Falcon	✓					✗	✓		✗		✓	✗
Beaver	✗					✓	✗	✓		✗		✓
Deer	✓	✗						✗	✓		✗	
Woodpecker		✓	✗	✓				✗	✓			✗
Salmon	✗		✓	✗					✗	✓		
Bear		✓		✓	✗						✗	✓
Raven	✓		✗		✓	✗		✓				✗
Snake	✗	✓		✗			✓	✗				
Owl		✗	✓		✗			✓	✗			
Goose			✗	✓			✗		✓	✗		

CHAPTER 2:
FALLING IN LOVE

Nothing is more blissful than the first days and weeks after you meet that special someone. Though it may be tempting to throw caution to the wind and let yourself be swept away by love, do not abandon reason altogether. Use the tools presented here to ascertain whether you and your partner are truly a good match and to see what lies in store for your unique love pairing.

THE PORTENTS OF THE FIRST DATE

The first date can foretell a lot about the future of a relationship. If your first date is still to come, read the following to learn what you might expect for the date itself and for the rest of your relationship.

❖ **Hallmarks of a relationship with a Monday first date:** Your relationship will be marked by fiery emotion but also a great deal of compassion for one another. You will have a happy domestic life, and your home will always be neat and tidy.

If you go on a first date on a Monday: Be prepared to be in touch with your feelings. If the date is going well, do not be afraid to visualize a future together. White is a good color to wear.

❖ **Hallmarks of a relationship with a Tuesday first date:** Self-assertion and fiery passion will be touchstones of your relationship. You will share great optimism about your life together.

If you go on a first date on a Tuesday: Tuesday is a good day for an active date or a date outdoors—consider roller skating, croquet, or boating. Wear red!

❖ **Hallmarks of a relationship with a Wednesday first date:** You and your mate will travel far and wide during your relationship but will also make a happy and peaceful home.

If you go on a first date on a Wednesday: Wear purple. It is likely you will skip the pleasantries and get right into intellectual conversations on the date.

❖ **Hallmarks of a relationship with a Thursday first date:** As a couple, you will invest wisely and will be prosperous. You will also be generous with your money and donate to those in need.

If you go on a first date on a Thursday: Consider a volunteer activity of some sort for your date. Blue is the best color to wear.

❖ **Hallmarks of a relationship with a Friday first date:** The two of you will always appreciate one another. You will find great beauty in your lives.

If you go on a first date on a Friday: Friday is a very fortuitous day for a first date. Wear green! A date that involves the arts will work best: a gallery opening, ballet recital, or theater performance.

❖ **Hallmarks of a relationship with a Saturday first date:** You and your partner will always protect each other and work in each other's best interests.

If you go on a first date on a Saturday: Wear black. A date that includes a project in which you both participate is advised. Perhaps a hands-on cooking class or a pottery-painting session?

❖ **Hallmarks of a relationship with a Sunday first date:** You and your mate will spend much fulfilling quiet time together. Meditation may be a part of your relationship.

If you go on a first date on a Sunday: Sunday is the sun's day—thus you should wear yellow. Make sure a walk out of doors is part of the date.

FACE READING FOR LOVE

Though you may be drawn to a mate based on physical appearance, you may not know that physical characteristics also serve as windows to a person's personality and behavior. The art of face reading, first used in ancient Greece and China, can explain the meaning behind certain features.

Three basic face shapes exist and carry with them different characteristics:

❖ **Round face (a round chin and full cheeks):** Round faces belong to people who tend to be friendly, sociable, intuitive, and hard-working. They like a happy home life filled with creature comforts.

❖ **Square face (a defined jaw and chin, and a wide forehead):** Those with square faces are dynamic personalities and born leaders. They are physically fit, active, capable, have strong opinions, and enjoy intellectual discussions.

❖ **Triangular/heart-shaped face (a larger forehead that narrows toward the chin):** Triangular faces generally belong to people who are more introverted; they are sensitive and prone to mood swings, but they are clever thinkers, loyal friends, and proceed always with a sense of purpose.

	ROUND FACE (WOMAN)
ROUND FACE (MAN)	Family will be paramount in this relationship, as will financial stability for the future. A good match.
SQUARE FACE (MAN)	A successful pairing so long as the Square man takes care not to completely overshadow the Round woman.
TRIANGULAR FACE (MAN)	If the Round woman can learn to anticipate and adapt to the Triangular man's changing moods, this relationship will succeed.

UARE FACE (WOMAN)	TRIANGULAR FACE (WOMAN)
s pairing is a happy one, ong as work and family are kept separate.	The Round man's natural joviality will draw the Triangular woman out of her shell, and he will be awed by her ambition and drive.
s union is marked by a verful mutual attraction; vever, both parties must e care to avoid battles vills.	This relationship is a fiery, powerful one. If both partners are able to stave off jealousy, they will be happy and will go far together.
e Triangular man in this ationship may find himself ninated by his partner imes.	This relationship will succeed because both partners have the same goals, though they may often disagree.

In addition to face shape, different aspects of the face cover different personality traits.

FOREHEAD

The forehead indicates intelligence. A sloped forehead represents a person who thinks quickly on his feet, while a narrow forehead is the sign of a person who needs to think things through long and hard before acting. A high forehead belongs to someone who will always need to be intellectually challenged, while a person with a wide forehead possesses creativity and practicality in equal measure.

EYEBROWS

The eyebrows indicate creativity, sociability, and a sense of pride. The higher the eyebrow, the more cautious the person. A highly arched brow indicates someone who is good with her hands, while a straight-browed person has an eye for beauty and a sensitive temperament.

EYES

The eyes indicate intelligence as well as openness to new experiences. Wide-set eyes likely belong to a dreamer who is tolerant of differences, while someone with close-set eyes is more narrow-minded but performs well under pressure.

EARS

The ears indicate decision-making ability and tolerance for risk. Small-eared people act swiftly and instinctively, while those with larger ears weigh all angles before making a decision. Ears that lay flat on the head point to a stable, frugal personality. On the other hand, a person whose ears stick out is likely a spontaneous individual who does not mind taking a chance.

CHEEKS

The cheeks indicate confidence. Those with high cheekbones are not easily swayed by the opinions of others. Prominent cheekbones point to a dominant personality but also a frugal nature. Narrow cheeks often belong to a stubborn and forceful individual, while wide cheeks are the mark of a more easygoing personality.

NOSE

The nose indicates opinions on money and family. One with a larger nose will be quite outgoing and enjoy large gatherings. If his nose is smaller, he'll be more reserved. A person with an upturned nose loves to interact with others, especially his kin. Someone with a snub nose can keep secrets well, while an individual with a more pointed nose has a strong will and a great desire for success in business.

MOUTH

The mouth indicates communication and expression. Large lips usually belong to individuals with expensive tastes but also stores of generosity, while a person with small thin lips may be more self-centered and unemotional. Lips that curve upward naturally point to an optimist with a cheerful, outgoing personality, while those with lips that curve downward are often hard to please.

TEETH

The teeth indicate patience and fastidiousness. A person with small teeth is careful and methodical in all his actions, while large front teeth generally belong to a strong individual, but one who is quite impatient. Space between the two front teeth points to a person who does not mind taking risks.

CHIN

The chin indicates assertiveness, determination, and willpower. The farther a chin sticks out, the more tenacious its owner tends to be. A sharp, pointed chin is the sign of great stamina and endurance, but also a degree of stubbornness and need for control. A small or undefined chin likely belongs to a peacemaker who prefers to avoid conflict.

BIRTHMARKS

As a general rule, birthmarks on the right side of the body are more fortuitous than those on the left.

A circle-shaped birthmark means good luck for its owner.

A birthmark on the leg portends overseas travel.

A birthmark on the arm connotes strength, both inner and outer.

A birthmark on the face will protect its owner's looks from fading in old age.

COWLICK

A person with a cowlick will have exceptional luck all his life. If it is a double cowlick, the luck also is doubled.

DIMPLES

A person blessed with dimples will maintain a cheerful personality in the face of adversity and will always be lucky in love.

MOLES

Moles are fortuitous signs of money and protection. Consider this old rhyme:

A mole on the neck,
You'll have money by the peck.
A mole on the ear,
You'll have money by the year.
A mole on the lip,
You're a little too flip.
A mole on your arm,
You'll never be harmed.
A mole on your back,
You'll have money by the sack.

Other mole portents include:

❖ **On the forehead or hairline:** Prosperity will rain down upon this person.

❖ **Between the eyebrows:** A person of great wisdom

❖ **On the nose:** An individual who is frugal now but will reap the rewards later

❖ **On the left cheek:** Success will come to this person after hard work.

❖ **On the right cheek:** Someone who seems studious and shy but has a wicked sense of humor underneath

WIDOW'S PEAK

A widow's peak is a sign of psychic powers.

SLEEPING POSITIONS AND THEIR MEANINGS

The way a person sleeps speaks volumes about who he is when he is awake. If your mate sleeps in more than one position, look to both meanings.

BACK SLEEPERS

Those who sleep on their back with their arms outstretched are good listeners and loyal friends, and they generally prefer for others to take center stage.

Back sleepers who keep their arms close to their body are generally reserved and hold themselves and others to high standards.

FETAL POSITION SLEEPERS

Those who sleep in the fetal position come across as tough and guarded but inside are quite sensitive.

SIDE SLEEPERS

People who sleep on their side with their arms out are tolerant and open-minded, although they can be quite stubborn.

Side sleepers who keep their arms close to their body are social and outgoing. However, they can be too trusting.

STOMACH SLEEPERS

Stomach sleepers are liked by all and have uncommon reserves of courage.

HANDWRITING FOR LOVE

The size, shape, and slant of a person's handwriting can tell you a lot about his character. As you are getting to know your new love better, take a look at his penmanship. If you have a love letter he has written you to use as a sample, all the better!

LETTER SIZE

❖ **Large:** One who prefers to stand out in a crowd; a gregarious, lively, bold, and unforgettable personality

❖ **Medium:** Someone who adapts well to all situations; a balanced and practical person

❖ **Small:** A humble, detail-oriented person who avoids the spotlight and has strong powers of concentration

LETTER SLANT

❖ **Strong right slant:** An impulsive personality who is always on the move; she is demonstrative, affectionate, and ruled by her emotions

❖ **Right slant:** A friendly and outgoing person who can set and achieve goals

❖ **No slant (letters are straight up and down):** A logical, practical thinker who controls her emotions

❖ **Left slant:** An observant individual; a good listener; a creative, original thinker

❖ **Varying slant (some left, some right):** A person of varying moods and unpredictable actions who is nonetheless extremely captivating to the opposite sex

BASELINE

(the imaginary line upon which letters and words sit)

- **Straight baseline:** A determined and self-motivated person who is not easily taken off his course

- **Ascending baseline (rises from left to right):** An optimistic and positive individual who sees the best in everyone and has high hopes for the future

- **Descending baseline (falls from left to right):** A hard worker, although she may be a bit pessimistic

- **Meandering baseline (rises and falls):** Someone who lacks direction and motivation

SIMPLICITY OF PENMANSHIP

- **Very straight letters with no flourishes at all:** A clear thinker who gets to the heart of the matter and tells it like it is; one who takes initiative

- **Fairly straight letters with some loops and flourishes:** Someone who relies upon common sense and close observation to make decisions; a practical, reliable person

- **Elaborate letters, with many curlicues and flourishes:** This person has been known to get caught up in unimportant details while ignoring the big picture; likely a magnetic personality and a compelling public speaker

KISSES AND THEIR PORTENTS

A kiss is one of the most direct ways to show affection for your mate. However, different kinds of kisses carry different meanings. Learn what your beloved is saying with his kiss and be aware of the message you yourself are sending.

KISS ON THE LIPS

The meaning of this classic kiss lies in its intensity. A quick peck on the lips may mean nothing more than "I want to be your friend," while a more lingering lip kiss implies passion, attraction, and possibly love.

KISS ON THE HAIR

A kiss on the top of the head represents a desire to nurture and protect one's love. Such kisses often take place when one partner is significantly older than the other or when there is a maternal or paternal element to the relationship.

KISS ON THE FOREHEAD

This kiss implies caring and generally is not a signal of physical attraction. In a more-established relationship, a kiss on the forehead can be a sign of deep affection, while in a newer relationship it can portend either affection or uncertainty. A kiss on the forehead may also symbolize that the giver feels protective of the recipient.

KISS ON THE CHEEK

A cheek kiss displays affection and support and can be flirty or friendly. Though it is often used as a greeting (to say hello or goodbye), kissing your mate on the cheek can be an unexpected way to show you care at any time.

KISS ON THE NOSE

A kiss on the nose is friendly and playful. If your mate kisses you on the nose, it is likely that you have a very relaxed relationship with much silliness and laughter. This type of kiss also signifies the comfort your love feels in your presence.

KISS ON THE EAR

This kiss can be mischievous and playful, or passionate and seductive, depending on the mood and your intent.

KISS ON THE SHOULDER

Kissing your loved one on the shoulder is a way to tell him that you think he is wonderful and a perfect match for you. For best effect, kiss his shoulder from behind while wrapping your arms around him.

KISS ON THE NECK

This is a very intimate kiss, and a clear sign of physical attraction. If your mate gives you this kiss, he is saying "I want more."

KISS ON THE COLLARBONE

A kiss on the collarbone is a seductive move; to kiss your lover here symbolizes the closeness between you and can serve as a prelude to more-intimate actions.

KISS ON THE HAND OR HANDS

This kiss shows great respect and tenderness. At the beginning of a relationship, a kiss on the back of a hand may signify a degree of formality on the part of the giver. In more established couples, the sentiments expressed by a kiss on the palm of a hand are adoration, admiration, and trust.

KISS WHILE CUPPING ONE'S FACE

If your lover kisses you and simultaneously cups her hand or hands around your face, she is saying "I can't live without you."

KISS WITH HAND ON WAIST

This kiss symbolizes a need on the part of the giver to hold on, both to the receiver and to the relationship.

KISS WITH CLOSED EYES

Those who kiss with closed eyes are romantic and secure in their relationship.

KISS WITH OPEN EYES

Those who kiss with their eyes open have a need to be in control and are often unable to give themselves over completely to love.

UPSIDE-DOWN KISS

Kissing your partner from above, so your top lip kisses his bottom lip and vice versa, signifies that you desire more spontaneity in your relationship. It can also be a very sensuous kiss because it is so unexpected.

ANGEL KISS

To give your partner an angel kiss, kiss her very gently on her eyelids or on her brow bone. This kiss expresses tenderness and a desire to care for your loved one.

BUTTERFLY KISS

A butterfly kiss does not involve the lips. Rather, two lovers draw close together so the tips of their eyelashes touch and then blink fast so the eyelashes flutter (like butterfly wings) and touch each other. In a solo butterfly kiss, one lover flutters her eyelashes against her mate's cheek or other body part. Butterfly kisses show playfulness as well as intimacy and can be shared by longtime lovers or new partners.

ESKIMO KISS

In an Eskimo kiss, two people rub their noses back and forth against each other. With eyes open, this kiss shows friendship or affection between couples; with eyes closed, it can be the prelude to more romantic kisses.

SIGNS YOU HAVE FOUND LOVE

Having used all the tools on the preceding pages to determine whether you and your mate are a good match, you may now be wondering how you know if true love has found you. Consider the criteria that follow.

Sure signs you are in love include:

❖ You feel relaxed, at ease, and most like your true self when you are with your mate.

❖ You can envision a future ahead as a couple.

❖ You trust your mate and know that he trusts you.

❖ You feel comfortable sharing secrets and less-than-flattering parts of yourself with your mate.

❖ You have eyes for no one but him.

❖ You feel that your mate makes you a better person, and you do the same for him.

❖ You are happiest when you are spending time together.

❖ You are proud of your mate, and you want to help him succeed in his endeavors.

❖ Your happiness as a couple is as important as your individual happiness.

❖ You feel that you and your mate complete each other.

CHAPTER 3:
BEING IN LOVE

Once you have found love, you will undoubtedly want it to last forever. But how your love endures is directly related to the effort you put into it. Whether this effort takes the form of spells and rituals you perform with your mate, gifts you give each other, foods you eat to spice up your love life, or many more matters, here is the wisdom you need to keep your love burning bright for years to come.

GIFTS OF LOVE

Gifts are imbued with deep portent. When you give (or receive) a gift of love, find its meaning here.

❖ **Artwork:** Our love will endure.

❖ **Belt:** I want you near me always.

❖ **Book:** You are in my heart and my mind.

❖ **Candle, lamp, or other light:** You are my beloved.

❖ **Candy or chocolate:** I want our love to endure.

❖ **Coat:** I want to care for you.

❖ **Doll:** I hope you remember me always.

❖ **Eyeglasses or sunglasses:** I want to see the true you.

❖ **Flowers:** You are beautiful.

❖ **Gloves**: I will always be truthful and faithful.

❖ **Handkerchief:** If we are separated, I will always wait for you.

❖ **Hairpins or hair adornments:** Above all else, I wish success for you.

- **Hat:** I want you to return my love.

- **Keychain:** I wish you good luck.

- **Mirror:** Do not forget me.

- **Necklace:** I want you to be by my side.

- **Nightgown or sleepwear:** I am yours.

- **Pen or other writing implement:** I will help you succeed.

- **Picture frame:** Please remember me.

- **Scarf:** I want our love to last forever.

- **Umbrella:** I will protect you.

- **Watch:** I cherish you.

WELSH LOVE SPOONS

Beginning in the sixteenth century, Welsh young men carved spoons with intricate designs out of a single piece of wood and presented them to their sweethearts. The motifs in the designs carried meaning and endure to this day. So if you receive a gift of any kind that contains these motifs, even if your love did not create it himself, you will know what it means.

- ❖ **Balls in a cage:** May we have as many children as there are balls in this cage.

- ❖ **Bell:** I want to marry you.

- ❖ **Bird:** I want to run away with you.

- ❖ **Chain:** May we be together forever.

- ❖ **Diamond:** May money and good fortune be ours.

- ❖ **Dragon:** I will protect you.

* **Flower:** My affection knows no bounds.

* **Heart:** I love you.

* **Horseshoe:** Luck will always be on our side.

* **Key:** I will always care for you.

* **Knot:** Our love is eternal.

* **Twisted stem:** Two will become one.

* **Wheel:** I will do whatever it takes to win your love.

ANIMAL IMAGERY IN LOVE GIFTS

Animals carry omens and hold meaning when they appear in gifts of love.

❖ **Bird:** Love

❖ **Cat:** Luck

❖ **Dog:** Loyalty

❖ **Fish:** Fertility

❖ **Frog:** Patience

❖ **Hen:** Domesticity

❖ **Lion:** Bravery

❖ **Tortoise:** Protection

THE MEANING OF FLOWERS

Just like other gifts, flowers (as well as plants and herbs) hold specific meaning when presented as tokens of love. When arranged together, your bouquet can send the perfect message to your beloved.

❖ To pledge commitment to your desired, present her with a bouquet of blue violets for fidelity, heliotropes for devotion, and clover for promise.

❖ If you and your love have been parted, send a bouquet with pansy and petunia for reassurance and comfort, evening primrose for silent love, and forsythia for anticipation.

❖ To seal your long-lasting love for your beloved, give him a bouquet of basil for enduring love, forget-me-not for faithfulness, hollyhock for all-consuming love, and honeysuckle for unity.

❖ To remind your loved one of the passion in your relationship, gather a bouquet of irises for ardor, periwinkle for closeness, jonquil for desire, and azalea for romance.

❖ An appropriate bouquet for young lovers includes lilac and freesia for innocence, aster for delicate love, and chrysanthemum for optimism.

❖ If your love is doubting your feelings are true, give her an arrangement of tulips for devotion, sunflower for adoration, wormwood for requited love, and sweet pea for lasting love.

❖ To thank your love for what she has brought to your life, present her with a bouquet of flax for gratitude, camellia for loveliness, and alyssum for worth beyond beauty.

❖ To show your beloved that you believe in him, give him a bouquet of narcissus for respect, hyacinth for admiration, and chive for good luck.

❖ If you are experiencing trying times in love, gather a bouquet for your love of acorn for strength, almond blossom for hope, cranesbill for constancy, and peony for renewal.

❖ To remind your love of her beauty inside and out, a good combination of flowers is dahlia for elegance, camellia for loveliness, alyssum for worth beyond beauty, and cherry blossom for feminine power and beauty.

❖ If you wish to show your mate that you will keep your word, present him with a bouquet of clover for promise, heliotrope or hydrangea for devotion, and petunia for reassurance.

THE ROSE: LOVE'S FLOWER

The rose, the flower most strongly associated with love, has meaning and portent all its own based on the many different colors in which it can appear.

- ❖ **White or ivory:** Romance and lasting love, new beginnings

- ❖ **Pale pink:** Dreamy first love

- ❖ **Dark pink:** Gratitude

- ❖ **Peach:** Admiration and sincerity

- ❖ **Coral:** Affection and desire

- ❖ **Fuchsia or magenta:** Passion and daring

- ❖ **Red:** True love, lust, and romance

- ❖ **Burgundy or deep red:** A stormy yet passionate love

- ❖ **Purple:** Passion, power

- ❖ **Lavender:** Love at first sight

- ❖ **Blue:** A unique love

❖ **Pale green:** Fertility and good luck

❖ **Yellow:** Happiness

❖ **Orange:** Passion and energy

❖ **Red and white roses together:** Unity

❖ **Roses without thorns:** "I hope"

MYTHOLOGY OF THE ROSE

How exactly did the beauty of the rose and its intoxicating perfume come about? Myths from many cultures hold that tragic stories of love led to the rose's creation, and thus it has been a flower forever linked to lovers.

RODANTHE AND DIANA

In Roman times, Rodanthe was an exquisite beauty, pursued by many suitors. But she wanted none of them, and she hid in the temple of the goddess Diana. The suitors would not be put off, and so they broke through the temple gates to get at Rodanthe. Enraged, Diana turned Rodanthe into a white rose and all her suitors into thorns. From that day forward, the rose has been a symbol of love.

CUPID

Legend has it that Cupid is responsible for the fact that roses have thorns. One day, while Cupid was aiming his arrow, he was stung by a bee, causing him to flinch and miss his target. Instead, his arrow pierced a bed of roses, and thereafter they grew thorns.

CHLORIS AND APHRODITE

A Grecian nymph named Chloris stumbled upon a lifeless fellow nymph while walking in the woods one day. She was heartbroken and pleaded with Aphrodite, the Greek goddess of love, to revive her friend. Aphrodite refused but said she would make the nymph everlasting and turned her into a beautiful flower—the rose. Aphrodite asked the god of wine, Dionysus, to give the rose a beautiful nectar and aroma. Zephyr made the winds blow the clouds away, and Apollo, the god of sun, shone down on the rose so it bloomed. Hereafter, the rose was considered the flower of gods and goddesses.

VENUS AND ADONIS

Venus, the Roman goddess of love and beauty, fell in love with a mortal named Adonis. Tragically, he was killed while hunting. As Venus wept for him, her tears fell to the earth and caused white roses to bloom. Her eyes blurred by tears, she stumbled into a garden of thorns. The thorns pricked her feet, and her blood fell upon some of the white roses, coloring them red.

THE NIGHTINGALE

In Persian mythology, red roses were created when a nightingale, who loved a white rose, swooped down upon it, piercing himself in the breast with one of its thorns. The bird's blood stained the white rose red.

GIFTS OF JEWELRY

Precious metals and gemstones hold the power to change situations—a power that is amplified if they are given as gifts of love.

❖ **Amber:** Changes negative feelings to positive ones

❖ **Amethyst:** Calms the mind; brings clarity and wisdom

❖ **Aquamarine:** Brings courage and offers protection and strength

❖ **Carnelian:** Banishes envy and brings opportunities

❖ **Citrine:** Attracts success and wealth

❖ **Diamond:** Offers protection

❖ **Emerald:** Brings patience

❖ **Garnet:** Gives passion, constancy, stability

❖ **Gold:** Brings good health and willpower

❖ **Hematite:** Calms anxiety

❖ **Jade:** Offers serenity and prosperity

❖ **Lodestone:** Attracts love

❖ **Moonstone:** Amplifies feminine power

❖ **Onyx:** Brings stability

❖ **Opal:** Clarifies buried feelings and desires

❖ **Pearl:** Scares off sadness; brings joy

❖ **Peridot:** Brings understanding and acceptance; relieves fear and jealousy

❖ **Platinum:** Offers protection

❖ **Rose quartz:** Draws love and passion; opens the heart; allows free exchange of love

❖ **Ruby:** Heightens self-confidence

* **Sapphire:** Increases insight, intuition, and communication

* **Silver:** Prompts creative juices to flow and ushers in prosperity

* **Tigereye:** changes anxiety into confidence, motivation, and action

* **Topaz:** Brings on physical stamina and increases fidelity

* **Turquoise:** Creates a grounding presence; attracts prosperity

ANNIVERSARY GIFTS

It is a long-practiced custom, dating back to the Victorian era, to bestow gifts upon married couples for each milestone year they have been wed. Even if you are not yet married, the following gifts are time-less and wonderful tokens of love. For example, you could celebrate the date of your first meeting, or the anniversary of your first kiss, with a gift to your mate.

YEARS OF MARRIAGE	TRADITIONAL
1	Paper
2	Cotton
3	Leather
4	Fruit or flowers
5	Wood
6	Sugar, candy, or iron
7	Wool or copper
8	Bronze or pottery
9	Pottery or willow
10	Tin or aluminum
15	Crystal
20	China
25	Silver
30	Pearl
35	Coral
40	Ruby
45	Sapphire
50	Gold
55	Emerald
60	Yellow diamond
70	Platinum
75	Diamond, gold

MODERN	FLOWERS
Clocks	Carnation
China	Lily of the valley
Crystal	Sunflower
Appliances	Hydrangea
Silverware	Daisy
Wood	Calla lily
Desk sets	Freesia
Linens or lace	Lilac
Leather	Bird of paradise
Diamond jewelry	Daffodil
Watches	Rose
Platinum	Aster
Silver	Iris
Diamond	Lily
Jade	
Ruby	Gladiolus
Sapphire	
Gold	Yellow rose and violet
Emerald	
Diamond	
Platinum	
Diamond, gold	

RITUALS TO SAFEGUARD LOVE

Though your love is undoubtedly strong, performing a few of these rituals for extra protection cannot do any harm.

❖ Tie a strand of your hair to that of your lover's with a red ribbon. Wear it near your heart. He will never stray.

❖ Find a laurel twig or branch; break it in half as evenly as you can. Keep one half for yourself and give the other half to your love. As long as you hold on to your halves, both of you will be always faithful.

❖ Sit with your lover on a Friday and share wine from the same glass, while summoning the spirit of Aphrodite and asking her to protect and bless your love. If you do not finish the wine, pour it on the ground, not down the drain.

❖ To seal your love, kiss your partner outdoors, under a new moon.

❖ Hold a freshly picked sprig of mint in your palm and have your mate clasp her hand to yours. Press your hands together, without speaking, until the mint is warm.

❖ If you are drinking tea with your love, pour the tea, then put sugar in the cup, then milk. Proceeding in this order will make your love everlasting.

❖ Never look at the full moon together through a window or a looking-glass; this is bad luck for love.

❖ Sew a swan's feather into your mate's pillow (or slip it inside the pillowcase), and he will be yours for life.

❖ Take care never to singe the hair of your love, for this may extinguish the passion in the relationship immediately.

❖ Knit or crochet your beloved a hat or a scarf and weave one of your own hairs into it. He will then think of you fondly wherever he goes. (However, note that some believe it is bad luck to knit for someone unless you have been a couple at least a year.)

FENG SHUI FOR LOVE

Whether you and your mate share a dwelling or live apart, using the classic Chinese tradition of feng shui can ensure that love will continue to flow through the rooms of your home.

KITCHEN

Copper pots increase the flow of love in a relationship. Hang them in your kitchen.

Place herbs and spices in the southwest corner of the kitchen; this will keep the passion in your relationship alive.

BATHROOM

Hang a round mirror in the bathroom, as this will reflect the unity and completeness in your relationship back to you.

LIVING ROOM

Place items in pairs to signify your togetherness—two twin figurines on the mantel, two flowers in a vase, two matching chairs sitting opposite from one another, photographs of the two of you together.

BEDROOM

The bed should not face the door, for energy will flow out of it.

Do not have a mirror facing your bed—it brings the energy of other people into your bed and bedroom, even if those people are just reflections of you and your partner!

Place your bed in the center of the room, framed by two bedside tables to echo the balance of two people in a relationship and to provide equal opportunity for both partners. The bed should have a solid headboard to back up the relationship.

Remove any artwork or photographs in the bedroom that depict lone figures. Even if the images are of happy loved ones, they will bring loneliness and solitude to your relationship, instead of feelings of togetherness.

Do not perform any kind of exercise in your bedroom, for that exertion will carry over and make your love much more effortful.

By the same token, do not use your bedroom as a workspace.

During the day, keep blinds or shutters open to let light in. If the weather is temperate, keep the window cracked as well. This will revitalize the love energy in the room so your relationship feels forever fresh and new.

Place green plants in the bedroom to keep positive love chi (love energy) flowing.

CLOSETS

Be sure that closets have enough space for both partners' belongings, while still leaving some breathing room. His and hers closets are not a good idea.

THROUGHOUT THE HOME

The feng shui "love center" of the home is located in the far right corner of the home (from the front door). Give this area the strongest love chi possible by placing one or more of the following objects there:

✧ two pieces of rose quartz

✧ red candles

✧ two vases with real or silk flowers, or a pair of live plants

✧ a pair of bird figurines

Throughout your home, keep clutter to a minimum. A tidy home will keep stale, slow energy away.

Remove all reminders of past relationships, whether they are letters, clothing, or gifts from old loves. Simply keeping these objects can hinder your current relationship.

Finally, make sure all doors in your home open smoothly and quietly. Doors that squeak or scrape are blocking love energy.

FOODS AND HERBS FOR INCREASING LOVE

Certain edibles have the power to enhance feelings of love and otherwise positively affect relationships. Try one or more of the following suggestions if your love needs a boost.

BASIL

Folk legend holds that if a woman offers a basil plant to a man and he accepts it, he will love her forever more. Basil also engenders sympathy between people, and its scent promotes loving feelings. Finally, it purifies sacred spaces, like bedrooms.

CILANTRO

Cilantro, or coriander, hastens feelings of passion and love. Grinding the seeds into a powder, or muddling the leaves and decocting them in red wine creates a love potion that may guarantee an unforgettable evening.

CHILE PEPPER

Not surprisingly, chile peppers (both whole and dried, and in seed form) correspond to fiery energy and can be used to reignite the passion in a relationship. To keep your lover faithful, you can tie two dried chile peppers together with a red ribbon and put them underneath his pillow.

FIG

If your love bites into a fig while you are holding it, he will become even more infatuated with you.

KIWI

Eating kiwi, and feeding it to your mate, is a surefire way to spice up your love life.

LETTUCE

Lettuce arouses love, especially when two partners eat from the same leaf. It is also believed to enhance fertility.

MARJORAM

Marjoram is linked to the goddess Aphrodite, and legend holds that Aphrodite grew the herb in her garden on Mount Olympus and blessed it with a sweet fragrance. It stands for happiness in a relationship, especially when it comes to long-lasting love and relationships that endure. Its scent also promotes deep, happy sleep for couples.

PAPAYA

If you serve papaya to your mate, or eat it yourself, your feelings of devotion for one another will grow.

PLUMS AND PEACHES

Plums and peaches inspire constancy in a love affair. Eat them if emotions in your relationship have been up and down.

ROSE HIPS

You already know of the legendary power of the rose when it comes to love. Rose hips (the fruit of the rose plant) are no exception: they have extraordinary healing powers. Consume them in a tea if you and your love are having troubled times.

STRAWBERRY

The strawberry is linked to Freya, the Norse goddess of love; it represents sexuality and love. When shared by lovers, strawberries can safeguard a relationship.

THYME

Thyme is associated with Venus, who is in turn associated with love. Wearing a sprig of thyme in your hair or pinned to your clothing will make you especially attractive to your mate, though he may not be able to divine quite why he is so drawn to you. Thyme is also associated with courage, so you may consume it if you need to broach a tricky relationship topic.

VANILLA

Vanilla is also associated with Venus and love. Similar to thyme, vanilla has magnetic properties and can draw lovers together. Carry a vanilla bean with you or dab a bit of pure vanilla extract behind your ears and do not be surprised if your love finds you irresistible.

SOME OTHER FOODS THAT PROMOTE LOVE
ARE AS FOLLOWS:

❖ **Anise:** Builds fidelity

❖ **Cardamom:** Creates lust

❖ **Cinnamon:** Attracts love

❖ **Coriander:** Brings serenity and peace in love

❖ **Ginseng:** Creates lust

❖ **Lemongrass:** Draws pure love

❖ **Lemon verbena:** Purifies love

❖ **Sorrel:** Heals love's wounds

SPELLS FOR THE PROTECTION OF LOVE

The following spells will protect and enliven your relationship.

A SPELL TO SPICE UP A LOVE LIFE

This spell is best performed on a Friday or a Tuesday, during a waxing moon.

You will need:

❖ Red pepper flakes

❖ A red candle

❖ Matches

Sprinkle a pinch of the red pepper flakes on or around the candle. Light the candle and say the following:

Flames of love burn, with spicy red pepper
Boost desire and bring us together
Bring some passion between us two
An enchanted evening for me and you.

Let the candle burn for at least two hours.

A SPELL TO HEAL AN ARGUMENT

If you and your love have had a disagreement, try this simple spell to smooth things over. It is best performed on a Friday but can work any day of the week, especially if you have recently argued.

You will need:

❖ 2 tablespoons dried basil leaves

Sprinkle one quarter of the basil leaves in each corner of your home, walking in a clockwise direction. As you sprinkle, chant the following words:

Around my home I sprinkle these fragrant leaves,
Banish anger and negativity from these eaves.
May our feelings ease and our hearts stand fast
That the love between us may ever last.

A SPELL TO MAINTAIN FIDELITY

Use this spell if you wish your lover to always remain faithful. Perform it on the night of a full moon.

You will need:

❖ Four candles

❖ Sea salt

❖ Matches

Place the candles in the shape of a diamond, each one facing a different direction (due north, south, east, and west). Create a circle with sea salt that encircles the four candles. Light each candle.

Face east and say:

Winds of the east,
Goddess of the feast,
Keep [name of lover] *with me*
So may it be.

Face south and say:

Fires of passion,
Keep [name of lover] close to me
So may it be.

Face west and say:

Waters of our hearts
Never do part
So may it be.

Face north and say:

Goddess of the earth,
Keep [your name] and [your lover's name]
Together for now and ever more
So may it be.

Break the circle by pushing a small piece of sea salt away.
Let the candles burn until they naturally extinguish themselves and then bury them near your home.

A SPELL TO PROTECT AND GUARD
YOUR LOVE

Perform this spell to keep your love sacred.

You will need:

❖ Red or purple construction paper

❖ Scissors

❖ A photograph of you and your beloved

❖ Double-sided tape

❖ A red pen

❖ Rose oil

Cut the paper into a heart shape a bit larger than your photograph. Affix the photograph to the heart with the tape. Write the names of you and your beloved on the paper.

Dab the paper with the rose oil, chanting,

Rose of love, this charm has begun,
That I and [name of your beloved]
Will always be one!

SPELL FOR A HEALTHY RELATIONSHIP

Apples represent health, vanilla and cinnamon inspire love, and ginger is an aphrodisiac.

To perform the spell:

Find a recipe for an apple pie or apple crisp that includes vanilla, cinnamon, and ginger (or use your favorite recipe). As you are putting the pie in the oven, say these words:

Secured within, so my magic begins
Transform this pie with love, and bless us from above!

A SPELL TO MAKE LOVE LAST

This spell requires the participation of both partners and is a time-tested way to strengthen your bond. Perform this ritual on a Friday evening after you have had a particularly long week.

You will need:

❖ White candles

❖ Matches

❖ A basin

❖ Rose oil

❖ Sweet almond oil

❖ Gardenia oil

❖ Jasmine oil

❖ Neroli oil

❖ A piece of pink or red paper

❖ A pen

❖ 3 dried rose petals

Light the candles and place them around your bathroom, bedroom, or wherever the ritual is to take place. Your partner should prepare a basin of warm water with a few drops of rose oil and wash your feet in the basin by candlelight. While your feet are soaking, he should prepare a massage oil with two tablespoons of sweet almond oil and a drop each of gardenia oil, jasmine oil, and neroli oil.

While the massage oil is being prepared, you should take the piece of paper and write in the middle of it three qualities that you want to preserve or foster in your relationship—passion, understanding, communication, trust, and so forth. Next, write your name and your partner's name in a circle around the three qualities.

Sprinkle two drops of the massage oil onto the paper and place the rose petals on top. Fold the paper in half and then in half again.

Your partner should then massage your feet using the remaining oil. Hold the paper in your hand while the massage is taking place and visualize the qualities you wrote down blooming forth in your relationship.

The next Friday, repeat the ritual again but trade places so your partner is the recipient of the massage.

LOVE RITUALS AROUND THE WORLD

Valentine's Day is not the only holiday for lovers. Consider instituting some of the traditions from other cultures into each year of your love.

BRAZIL

Dia dos Namorados (Boyfriends' and Girlfriends' Day) occurs on June 12. On and around this day, single women perform rituals called *simpatias*, which they hope will help them find a boyfriend or husband. In Portugal, a similar celebration takes place, but it occurs on April 23, St. George's Day.

DENMARK

On Valentine's Day, Danes send snowdrops (white flowers) to their friends. Another custom holds that a Danish man sends a valentine card known as a *gaekkebrev* (loosely translated as a "joker letter") to the object of his desire. He writes a rhyme or a note in the card, and instead of signing his name, simply writes one dot for each letter in his name. It is then up to the recipient to guess his identity. If she can do so, he will reward her with a gift of an Easter egg later in the year.

ISRAEL

The fifteenth day of the month of Av (usually sometime during August) is the traditional Jewish festival of love. In olden days, girls would don white dresses and dance in vineyards on this day, and boys would watch them. Matchmaking followed. Today, it is a popular date for proposing marriage.

JAPAN

On Valentine's Day, Japanese women give chocolates to men. One month later, on March 14, Japanese celebrate "White Day," in which the men return the favor to women.

KOREA

The fourteenth of every month is a love holiday in Korea. From January to December, they are Candle Day, Valentine's Day, White Day, Black Day, Rose Day, Kiss Day, Silver Day, Green Day, Music Day, Wine Day, Movie Day, and Hug Day.

ROMANIA

Romania's holiday of love is called Dragobete, named after a character in folklore, and is celebrated on February 24.

SPAIN

Those who live in Catalonia celebrate La Diada de Sant Jordi (St. George's Day) on April 23, and they give roses and books to their loved ones.

TAIWAN

Just as in Japan, Taiwanese lovers celebrate Valentine's Day on February 14 and White Day on March 14. However, in a slight twist, men give gifts to women on February 14, and women present men with gifts one month later. In Taiwan, July 7 of the lunar calendar is also recognized as a love holiday, and men purchase roses for their sweethearts, believing that the number of roses sends a message. One red rose means "You are my only love"; 11 roses means "You are my favorite"; 99 roses means "I want to be with you forever"; and 108 roses is a marriage proposal.

NAMES OF THE HAPPY COUPLE

_____

and

_____

Date we met

_____

Library of Congress Cataloging-in-Publishing Data available.

ISBN 978-1-4521-0859-9

Manufactured in China
Design by Cat Grishaver
Text by K. C. Jones
Typeset in Neutra and Memphis

Also available in this series: *Fortune-Telling Book of Names*,
Fortune-Telling Book of Dreams, *Fortune-Telling Book for Brides*,
Fortune-Telling Book of the Zodiac, *Fortune-Telling Birthday Book*,
and *Fortune-Telling Book for Moms-to-Be*.

5 7 9 10 8 6 4

Chronicle Books LLC
680 Second Street
San Francisco, CA 94107
www.chroniclebooks.com